MEET THE KEY WORKERS

WORKERS IN EDUCATION

BY

SHALINI VALLEPU

KidHaven PUBLISHING

Published in 2024 by
KidHaven Publishing, an Imprint of Greenhaven Publishing, LLC
2544 Clinton St., Buffalo, NY 14224

Written by: Shalini Vallepur
Edited by: John Wood
Designed by: Jasmine Pointer

Cataloging-in-Publication Data

Names: Vallepur, Shalini.
Title: Workers in education / Shalini Vallepur.
Description: New York : KidHaven Publishing, 2024. | Series: Meet the key workers | Includes glossary and index.
Identifiers: ISBN 9781534544420 (pbk) | ISBN 9781534544437 (library bound) | ISBN 9781534544444 (ebook)
Subjects: LCSH: Education-- Juvenile literature | Faculty (Education) -- Juvenile literature | Teachers -- Juvenile literature
Classification: LCC LB1775 V35 2024 | DDC 371.1 --dc23

Manufactured in the United States of America

CPSIA compliance information: Batch #CSKH24: For further information contact Greenhaven Publishing LLC at 1-844-317-7404.

Please visit our website, www.greenhavenpublishing.com. For a free color catalog of all our high-quality books, call toll free 1-844-317-7404 or fax 1-844-317-7405.

Find us on

Image Credits

All images are courtesy of Shutterstock.com, unless otherwise specified. With thanks to Getty Images, Thinkstock Photo and iStockphoto.

Cover – Monkey Business Images, SpeedKingz, Lordn, Nazarkru. 2–3 – JR-50. 4–5 – Spotmatik Ltd, Monkey Business Images. 6–7 – Monkey Business Images, wavebreakmedia, robuart. 8–9 – wavebreakmedia, MicroOne, Travel Stock, wavebreakmedia. 10–11 – Gvardgraph, Monkey Business Images, Peryn22, Mind Pixell. 12–13 – elenabsl, Monkey Business Images, Andrewshots. 14–15 – Monkey Business Images, AnnGaysorn, R.Bordo. 16–17 – naum, Siyanight, Dirk Ott. 18–19 – 4 PM production, sirtravelalot, wavebreakmedia, Altrendo Images, Robert Kneschke, Oxy_gen. 20–21 – Pixel-Shot, jongcreative, VectorShow, Robert Kneschke, Yuriy Golub, wee dezign. 22–23 – Marion M.3, CharacterFamily70, MaryDesy.

CONTENTS

Words that look like **this** can be found in the glossary on page 24.

HERE TO HELP

There are lots of jobs in the world and each one is different. Some jobs are always needed. The people who do these jobs are called key workers.

Key can sometimes mean needed and important.

Nurses are always needed to take care of us when we are ill.

Without key workers, we would not have the things we need to live safely, such as food and important **services**.

PEOPLE IN EDUCATION

Education is when we learn. Our teachers help us learn. There are lots of people who help us learn inside and outside of school.

Many of the people who work in education are key workers.

People in education make sure that we are learning things, but they also make sure we are fed, happy, and healthy.

IN THE CLASSROOM

At school, we often spend most of the day in a classroom with a teacher. A teacher is **trained** to teach us many different things. They plan our lessons and make sure we understand everything.

Teaching assistants are there to help teachers. They help to get things ready in the classroom and may even listen to us read.

LUNCHTIME!

A school cook is someone who plans and cooks meals for us to eat. They make sure there is healthy food for everybody.

Do you eat a hot lunch or a packed lunch at school?

Lunch staff help the cooks. They may **serve** us food and make sure we are well behaved. If we play outside during lunchtime, they will **supervise** us.

HELP AND SUPPORT

School nurses are there for us if we feel ill at school. They can give us **medicine** or look after us if we feel sick.

School counselors are there to listen to our feelings and talk through our problems. Anybody can speak to a school counselor. School counselors make sure that school is a safe place for everybody.

Social workers work with schools. Their job is to make sure we are kept safe and well when we are at school or at home.

You can ask any of your teachers about helplines if you need to.

A helpline is a service that people can call on the phone. Some helplines are run by counselors for children. We can call a helpline if we need to talk to someone.

AFTER SCHOOL

There is a lot of work to be done, even when school is finished! Cleaners make sure that the school is clean and tidy for everyone.

School caretakers look after the school building. They make sure things are working properly and fix anything that is broken. If your school has a playing field, a groundskeeper might look after it.

You can help cleaners and caretakers by being tidy during the day!

Drivers make getting to and from school easier, especially if your school is far away. Crossing guards help people cross roads on their walk to school.

Bus driver

Getting on the bus

Crossing guard

If your parents or **guardians** are busy after school, it is important that someone looks after you! Caregivers look after us. They make sure we are safe.

CLUBS

Joining a school club is a great way to make new friends! You can find a club that spends time doing one of your favorite things.

After-school clubs are run by teachers. You can do all sorts of activities, such as sports, reading, and **STEM subjects**.

LIVE AND LEARN

Many different people work hard to help us learn. Why not give a thank-you card to somebody who has helped you?

Now you know about some of the people who work in education! Can you match each job below to the right person?

Teaching assistant	School cook	Bus driver
Helps get things ready in the classroom	Plans and cooks healthy meals for lunchtime	Makes getting to and from school easier

GLOSSARY

guardians	people who look after someone but are not their parents
medicine	something used or taken to fight off diseases
serve	to get something ready and bring it to someone
services	tasks or actions that people pay other people to do, such as caring for older people, fixing things that are broken, or cleaning
STEM subjects	lessons in school that include science, technology, and math
supervise	to watch someone in order to make sure they are safe or doing what they are meant to do
trained	having been taught how to do a job

INDEX